To

a wonderful Daughter Saxo

From

Mom

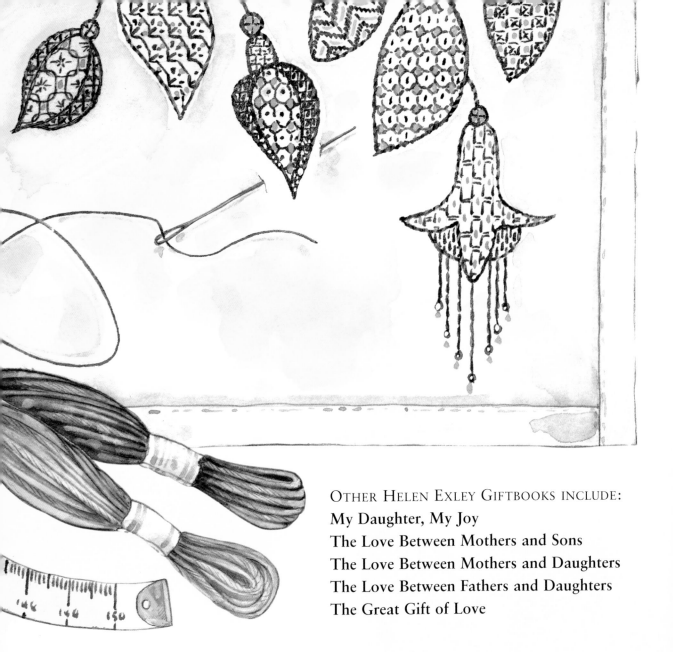

OTHER HELEN EXLEY GIFTBOOKS INCLUDE:
My Daughter, My Joy
The Love Between Mothers and Sons
The Love Between Mothers and Daughters
The Love Between Fathers and Daughters
The Great Gift of Love

This book has been created from the smaller *To a very special® Daughter* book published in Great Britain in 1991 by Helen Exley Giftbooks.
This enlarged edition first published in 2007. Copyright © Helen Exley 1991, 2007. The moral right of the author has been asserted.

To a very special® is a registered trademark of Helen Exley Giftbooks.

Dedication by Pam Brown: To my own dear daughters, Helen and Sarah and my extra daughter, Eve, from Mum.
With love and thanks and three rousing cheers.

12 11 10 9 8 7 6 5 4 3 2
ISBN 13: 978-1-84634-079-6

Edited by Helen Exley. Printed in China.

Helen Exley Giftbooks, 16 Chalk Hill, Watford, Herts WD19 4BG, UK
www.helenexleygiftbooks.com

To my very special
DAUGHTER

WRITTEN BY PAM BROWN
ILLUSTRATED BY JULIETTE CLARKE

A HELEN EXLEY GIFTBOOK

I often wondered before you came
how I would handle a daughter.
Did I want a frilly daughter
or a chunky, cheerful child?
Did I want her to be a celebrity?
Or caring? Or both?
As it was, I didn't get any of my dreams.
I got a totally unique,
totally new, totally puzzling,
unpredictable, delightful you.

. . .

"This is

I keep an album of photographs
of you – as if I could hold on
to all the different yous –
the baby, the toddler, the schoolgirl,
the teenager.
But they don't really matter.
Not that much.
Because you are all of them –
and every time I see you
I think, "This is the best time."

the best time"

Dear Daughter

Dear Daughter. I think of you all the time.

When I find the dye from your T-shirt has patterned

most things in the wash.

When I find long hairs in the drain pipe.

When I'm scrubbing the bath oil scum off the bath.

When I find a half-eaten bar of chocolate in your bed.

When I discover you've consumed all the ice-cream,

just before dinner.

When I find a yoghurt pot

full of primroses by my bed.

I love you.

Sometimes I wish

I had the power to make things come right for you.

Sometimes I wish I had money

enough to give you the things you dream of.

Sometimes I wish I had treasures to pass on to you.

But I gave what I could – your five bright senses,

the world about you.

Take what you want,

add your own wonder to the sum of all human wonder,

and pass on the gift of love.

It is enough.

Dear Daughter.

I wish you eyes to see – the gull's gawkish walk,

the turn of leaves,

the coil of running water,

the spurt of raindrops on a shining street,

rainbows, a swirl of starlings in a city sky.

I wish you ears to hear

– the murmur of hidden streams,

a morning robin, scufflings in the hedgerow,

the sound of traffic muted by summer trees,

anchor cable running out,

the hush of voices as the curtain rises.

Smells haunting and sharp,

enticing, evanescent.

The first violets, clean linen, roast chestnuts.

The touch of silk

and sun-warmed stone. Cats.

And familiar, loving hands.

The taste of new bread,

of clear water, of the vin du pays,

of a newly-picked tomato.

Dear Daughter – I wish you life.

I wish you life

Life's never dull!

Life since you came

has been like an extraordinary book

– one where I just can't wait

to turn the page

and see what new thing you have done.

I don't know which I like best

– the quiet chapters – or the big

dramatic scenes – or the cliff-hangers.

It's never dull.

I just can't get over the fact that

I had a hand in the authorship.

I'm proud of all your achievements.
You've worked hard for them.
I'm proud of your looks and your intelligence
– which some far distant ancestor handed down.
But I'm most proud of your being just you.
"Success" would be an extra
– but you are special to me
whatever you do.

I'm proud of you

not for the things that came easily to you –

or that were part of you from the very beginning

– but for your slogging it out

against the odds and against your nature

and spluttering to the surface

with your prize.

–whatever you do

You are unique

N o. You are not perfect

– and I am sorry

that when you were small I sometimes

seemed to demand perfection.

You are better than perfect.

You are a unique piece of humanity, fallible, questing,

always astonishing

in your discoveries and dreams.

I am everlastingly thankful

that a little of me

is caught up in your being, and that you

carry me into the future that I shall never know.

You are all of us

– and yet yourself forever.

...better than

perfect

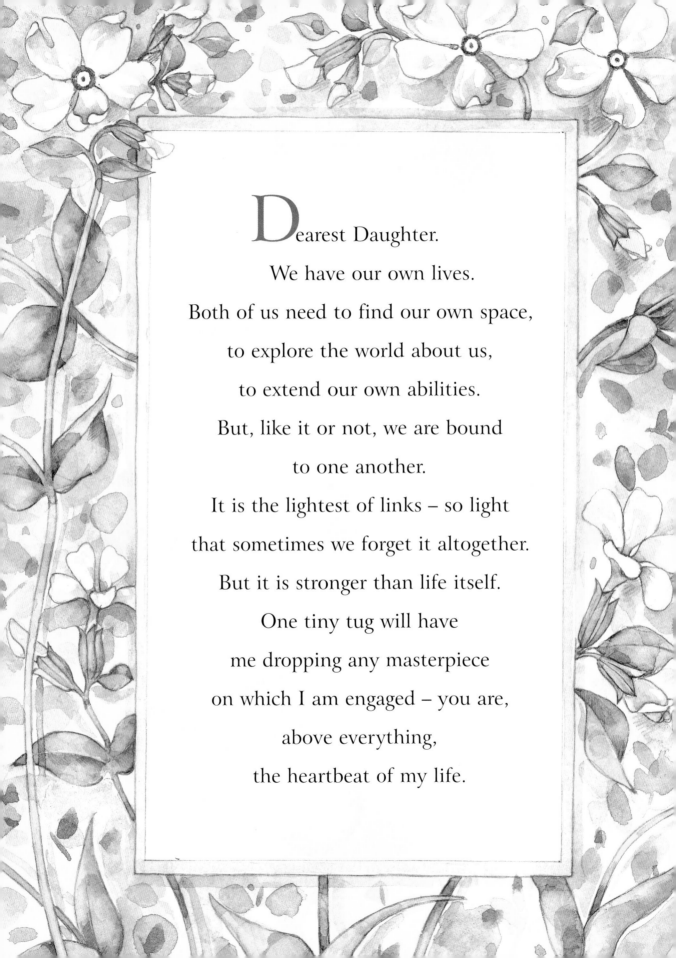

Dearest Daughter.

We have our own lives.

Both of us need to find our own space,

to explore the world about us,

to extend our own abilities.

But, like it or not, we are bound

to one another.

It is the lightest of links – so light

that sometimes we forget it altogether.

But it is stronger than life itself.

One tiny tug will have

me dropping any masterpiece

on which I am engaged – you are,

above everything,

the heartbeat of my life.

We've done well – seen wonders, dreamed dreams.

Perhaps we haven't made

a circumnavigation of the world, or climbed

Everest, or written a best seller. Yet.

We've different tastes, different skills,

different ambitions.

But we like to watch the other live and learn –

and to applaud when it's called for.

Perhaps we're not everyone's conventional idea

of a parent and daughter.

Perhaps there's no such thing.

But we like each other. We encourage each other.

We are friends.

We like each other

In a world where it is necessary
to succeed, perhaps only women
know more deeply
that success can be a quiet and hidden thing.

THANK YOU!

Thank you for having given me
the chance to make mud pies again,
to paddle in the sea, to sail toy boats,
to ride the fairground horses,
to try everything in the children's museum exhibit
– and to stroke all the goats in the children's zoo.

Thank you for an excuse
to play computer games and cook pizzas.
Thank you for bringing back fun to all our lives.

Thank you for believing

my birthday cakes were magical,

my paintings amazing

and my stories were the best in the world.

Sometimes

when I'm feeling particularly useless

you give me sound advice

– which I once gave to you.

It cheers me up no end.

Thanks for keeping an eye on me, Love.

Daughters are given to making announcements.

I'm joining an ashram.

I've signed on to crew a boat to Singapore.

I've invited my headteacher to dinner. Today.

I'm getting a tattoo. I'm leaving home.

I'm going to be a nun.

I'm in love with an Arab sheik.

I'm moving back home. I'm having my hair dyed green.

I'm going to settle down just as soon as

I've back-packed around Australia.

Having daughters is the best investment

you will ever make against becoming bored.

*A daughter
is a new
beginning*

Because of you,
I still see every day with a clearer eye
– as if for the very first time.

. . .

A daughter is a new beginning.
A daughter means
that you will know the meaning
of the verb To Worry.

A daughter is

your excuse for making a doll's house.

A daughter spells out the end of monotony.

A daughter is the one

who feathers her new nest

with feathers from your old one.

A daughter is the person you thought

you would stop worrying about

when she hit twenty-one.

But who is still worrying you silly at forty-five.

A daughter is your part in forever.

I could say you were the cleverest,

the most beautiful,

the most perceptive, even-tempered,

wise, considerate daughter

in the entire universe.

But that wouldn't be right.

I've not met all the daughters in the universe.

I can only judge

by my limited acquaintance.

But on that basis I say

you are the cleverest,

the most beautiful, the most...

I would be very proud if you were

an eminent brain surgeon or an acclaimed novelist

or a prima ballerina assoluta.

We parents would all love to refer casually

to, "My Daughter, the architect"

– or "the airline pilot."

But how can that better the pride

I have in you as you are –

whatever you achieve.

I look about me at a world grown

more dangerous than the one I had to contend with

– a world more ruthless, mad, greedy

and fragmented. Yet you cope with it.

*So very
proud of you*

I am proud of your kindness
and good sense,
your courage
and integrity and intelligence.
Use them in whatever way
you choose
– I am so very proud of you.

A child gives us
our own first times,
all over again.
I have watched the marvel
of a curtain-rise in your face,
the hushing of a concert hall
as the baton lifts,
the first sight of the sea.
Thank you
for reawakening wonder.

Reawakening wonder

When you were born, you were an amazement,

a perfection, a wonder.

We two most ordinary people had produced a marvel.

You opened your eyes,

and we knew you were already

your own person

– and a small shiver of wonder ran through us.

As you grew and smiled and began to speak

every day brought a new delight.

Every day

You walked and talked and we were enchanted.

But all the time you were turning

from our dream into your own reality. Yourself.

You grew older – and with the years

came measles and miseries,

confrontations over the height of heels,

the necessity of homework,

mud on the carpet, lost sports gear, first love,

and examinations

that sent us all gibbering to the edge.

a new delight

My hope for you
is that all your life you will go on
being astonished and delighted
by the world about you.

Of course I dream
I could give you all the places
I couldn't take you – Florence and Venice
and Rome, Paris
and Prague, the Isles of Greece,
St. Petersburg.
But you might not want them.
I wish you your own places,
your own adventures,
your own loves.

Dearest –

with all these technical wonders around us

I'm going to wish you

something incredibly old fashioned.

The joy of reading books.

Books unmolested by Hollywood, Theme Parks,

Digests or Strip Cartoonists.

Just books.

One mind speaking to another across time

and space.

My hopes
and dreams
for you

Daughters are a delight.

Some of the time.

Most of the time.

When, that is, they are not putting their

white ballet tights into the wash inside black jeans;

when they are not discovering

they haven't one clean shirt –

three minutes before the school bus leaves;

when they are not sitting in front of the dictionary,

vowing they can't find any word like aggravating.

And that they hate tomato sandwiches

and always have done.

Though they devoured

an entire plateful at last week's party....

April 5.
S.W.A.L.K.
my love
M. Barbosa,
Lower Farm,
Nalton St.
You are invited to.....
May 21
me for
lunch 12.0'clock
Sat 26th
be a

With you away adventuring,

the house seems

very flubsy and dull.

My mind half makes plans to go to sea again,

or cross the Sahara in a Land Rover or some such.

But then I catch sight of myself

in the mirror and I realize sadly

that my shinning-up-the-rigging

and brewing-up camp days are over.

You'll just have to do it for me.

Have as much fun and excitement

as I did. Boil the water. Shake the bedding.

Keep your feet in good order.

And write your diary.

My mind and heart are with you.

Have fun!

Thank you

Thank you for wilting dandelions,

for twigs of lamb's-tails, for wet pebbles,

for fluff-covered toffees, for sticky kisses.

Thank you for loving me.

Some daughters give florists' bouquets,

Cartier watches and Cointreau.

Some daughters send

shrubs, sweaters and home-made jam.

The thing is – daughters know

exactly what one needs.

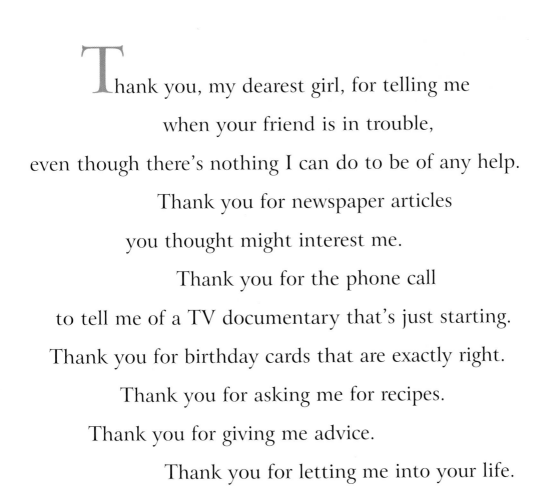

Thank you, my dearest girl, for telling me

when your friend is in trouble,

even though there's nothing I can do to be of any help.

Thank you for newspaper articles

you thought might interest me.

Thank you for the phone call

to tell me of a TV documentary that's just starting.

Thank you for birthday cards that are exactly right.

Thank you for asking me for recipes.

Thank you for giving me advice.

Thank you for letting me into your life.

for everything!

Ragings, weepings and the occasional

all-defying sulk.

But always, thank heavens, the flicker of hope

that it would all come right in the end.

Always the glimpse of the old magic

– the loving heart, the gift of laughter,

the joy of giving, the longing to explore

the world about you.

And all of it has combined to make you

what you are. Our dear daughter.

Our wise, determined daughter.

Our awkward, argumentative, aggravating

special daughter.

Our loving – and most dearly loved lass.

When we're apart...

There is nothing, absolutely nothing
that can cheer up
a dismal evening of TV repeats
and yesterday's leftovers
more successfully
than a phone call from a daughter.

Thank you for not letting the miles
diminish our friendship –
for always writing, however busy your schedule,
for phoning from strange places
and e-mailing pictures,
for little boxes of wedding cake,
for foreign newspapers and travel-worn parcels –
for making the world
seem companionable,
and the Andes just next door.

When you were very small
I could kiss most things better.
Or quietly, gently rock you to sleep.
I could mend most things
that a kiss couldn't cure
– with glue and tape, a needle and thread,
elastic, staples, string.
I was very good at replacing dolls' eyeballs

Always here

– and arms and legs. And hair.

But now there are things I cannot stick together,

or heal with a hug.

Grown-up matters beyond my skills.

I wish I had some magic

that could make such things come right.

All I can do is be here. Always.

for you...

Do you remember?

Do you remember

– walks through spring woods?

Winter mornings,

dark and cold and rustling?

The first day away,

walking to a shining sea

and the sound of the gulls?

Lopsided birthday cakes?

I do, I do.

When the world was new...

All the time, very quietly, daughters are changing.

Before long, you are

waving goodbye to them at the school gates.

A moment more and you have a teenager on your hands.

A flicker of time and they are leaving home

– an independent woman.

But they always hold within them

the little child that they once were.

Not just the memories of happiness and fears

– of buttercup meadows

and the grasses high above their heads, of secret places.

But all those times beyond recall,

when the world was very new

and there was everything to learn.

I wish you happy and secure
and comfortable and wise.

But not yet. Get the adventures in first!

My wishes for you,

I wish you the passion that creates
and pray the passion that destroys
passes you by.

How can I wish you anything?
Save that you find what you want to do
and do it. Well.

I wish you love. Romance, yes.

But, too, the love of those who lie together

in the darkness, talking of times past.

The reaching up of children's arms,

the honey-sticky kisses.

The butt of a small cat's head.

A dog's companionable sigh.

The reassuring touch, the lighting up of eyes,

the sound of a key in the lock.

my daughter

I wish you a daughter just like you.

I wish you the beauty of silence,
the glory of sunlight, the mystery
of darkness,
the force of flame, the power of water,
the sweetness of air, the quiet
strength of earth,
the love that lies at the very root of things.
I wish you the wonder of living.

What do I most wish for you?
A belief in the fundamental worth of humankind,
and that, my dear, includes yourself.

The wonder of living

*Friends and love
in abundance!*

No, Love, I don't dream
of wealth and success for you.
Only a job you like,
skills you can perfect,
enthusiasm to lighten your heart,
friends and love in abundance.

Dear. I hope that when you are very,
very old you can look back and say
"Heavens. That was a lovely life."

You have my love
– the love that links us.
Take it with you into the world
that I will never know.

You have my love